Artistic Elephants

By Heather Hammonds

T0342777

Contents

Elephants That Paint

Some animals are able to paint and draw. They are animal artists.

Elephants are able to paint and draw. There are elephant artists in zoos and refuges all around the world.

Many paintings by elephant artists are sold by zoos and animal charities. Some zoos and charities hold art exhibitions so people can see the paintings. The money raised by selling the paintings is used to help look after the elephants.

In some countries, elephants help clear forests. The timber from the forests is then sold by big timber companies. Elephants pull huge logs through the forests. They are made to work very hard in hot conditions.

Today, there are not as many forests so the elephants and their keepers have very little work.

Sometimes, the elephants are abandoned. They have no food and begin to starve.

feeding an abandoned baby elephant at a rescue centre

Elephant sanctuaries help care for abandoned and starving elephants. They also help the keepers that have no work by giving them jobs as caretakers.

caretakers bathing elephants at a sanctuary

Elephants are given paintbrushes and paints, and are taught how to paint. Their paintings are sold to tourists.

Elephant artists use a wide range of colours and have different painting styles, just as human artists do.

There are many beautiful examples of elephant art around the world.

Carol the elephant artist, San Diego Wildlife Park, California, USA

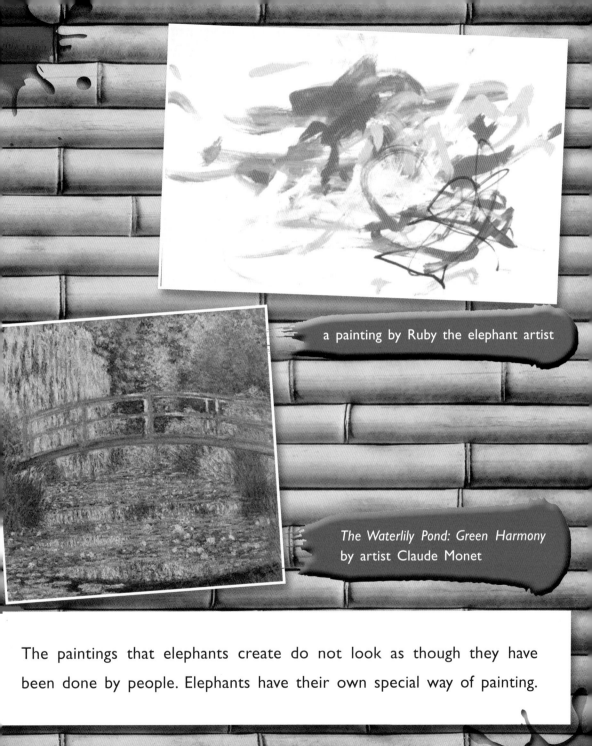

a painting by Ruby the elephant artist

The Waterlily Pond: Green Harmony
by artist Claude Monet

The paintings that elephants create do not look as though they have been done by people. Elephants have their own special way of painting.

Should Elephants Paint?

Letters to the Editor

Support our elephant artists

Everyone should go to the zoo and see the new Animal Art exhibition.

It is interesting to watch the elephants hold brushes in their trunks and create paintings for the exhibition.

Elephants are very intelligent animals and learning to paint helps stop them becoming bored at the zoo.

The zoo sells the elephants' paintings at the exhibition and on the Internet. The money raised is being used to build a larger enclosure for the elephants.

Because of this, the elephants will have a bigger and better home.

The Animal Art exhibition is a very good idea.

From Brett Cowling

building an elephant enclosure

Elephants should not paint

In reply to Brett Cowling's letter, I strongly disagree with the Animal Art exhibition currently being held at the zoo.

Elephants in the wild do not create paintings. I believe zoo elephants should do similar activities to wild elephants, whenever possible. They would be much happier as a result.

wild elephants

Perhaps the zoo could find other ways to raise funds to build a new elephant enclosure, such as asking for donations or holding a raffle.

To sum up, we should not teach zoo animals to paint and we should not sell their paintings to raise money.

From Jade Jackson